Your Dog and the Law

BY THE SAME AUTHOR
AND PUBLISHED BY SHAW & SONS:

THE DOG LAW HANDBOOK

ANIMAL LAW

GUN LAW

YOUR DOG AND THE LAW

BY
GODFREY SANDYS-WINSCH

B.A. (Cantab.) Solicitor

THIRD EDITION

Shaw & Sons Limited

Sponsored by Hill's Pet Nutrition Ltd.

Trusted by vets throughout the world*

Published by Shaw & Sons Limited
Shaway House
21 Bourne Park
Bourne Road
Crayford
Kent DA1 4BZ

© Shaw & Sons Limited 1993

ISBN 0 7219 1012 2

First published — September 1984
Second Edition — May 1990
Third Edition — June 1993

A CIP catalogue record for this book is available
from the British Library

Printed in Great Britain by
Bell & Bain Ltd., Glasgow

Contents

Preface to Third Edition

The publication of this edition comes earlier than would have been the case without the enactment of the Dangerous Dogs Act 1991 and the parts of the Environmental Protection Act 1990 dealing with stray dogs and dogs' excreta. These are the only significant changes in the law which have occurred since 1989.

The 1991 Act was quickly pushed through Parliament in the summer of that year following an increasing number of serious attacks by dogs on people, mainly by pit bull terriers, and the publicity given to them. It is too soon yet to assess its effectiveness, but early indications are that the problems of proving a dog to be of the breed alleged will cause serious difficulties in enforcement.

I am again grateful for the helpful advice from the Ministry of Agriculture, Fisheries and Food on updating the rules about the import of dogs. I am grateful, too, for the help received from the Department of the Environment on the 1990 Act and from the Home Office on the 1991 Act.

The law remains that of England and Wales, though applying also to Scotland in some instances.

Those readers requiring more detailed information on the aspects of law covered in this book are referred to *The Dog Law Handbook*, described on page 86.

Godfrey Sandys-Winsch
  Leasingham,
  Lincolnshire.

Preface to First Edition

I have written this booklet in the hope that it will prove useful, not only to dog owners, but also to others who may have cause to be involved with the law about dogs. In writing it, I have had two objectives in mind: to bring together concisely all the law pertaining to dogs; and to present that law in a readily understandable form, but admitting that, like most branches of the law, that law is not straightforward in some parts by reason of the way in which it is framed and that uncertainty exists in other parts.

I have chosen not to encumber the booklet with comprehensive references to statutes, statutory regulations and law cases, but have referred generally to the main statutes involved and have brought in case law anonymously, where it is relevant.

I wish to thank Mr. Dick Bowgen, firstly, for conceiving the idea of this booklet and, secondly, for his assistance with matters of pedigree. I am also grateful for the ready and comprehensive advice from the Ministry of Agriculture, Fisheries and Food on the import and export of dogs.

The law is that of England and Wales, though applying to Scotland also in some instances.

Godfrey Sandys-Winsch
Leasingham,
Lincolnshire.

Chapter 1

OWNERSHIP AND THEFT

Dogs, being domestic animals, are owned in the same way as inanimate objects such as cars and furniture. Ownership is retained when a dog is lost and, subject to the statutory rules in Chapter 9, when it strays. An owner whose dog is detained without the owner's permission by another person may sue that person in court for its return. He may also lawfully retake the dog from that person; although the law says that he is justified in the use of reasonable force if that person resists him, force should be used with caution because of possible ensuing complications.

The keeping and feeding of another person's dog does not by itself permit retention of the dog until its keep is paid.

Puppies are owned by the owner of their mother, unless there is a special agreement to the contrary.

It naturally follows from what has been said about ownership that a dog may be the subject of theft – though, strangely, this was not the case until 1968. Basically, a dog will be stolen when it is taken from its owner, or anyone else who has possession or control of it, with the intention of permanently depriving that person of it. A dog may also be the subject of offences associated with theft, such as obtaining property by deception and receiving stolen goods.

It is an offence to advertise publicly a reward for the return of a dog stolen or lost using any words to the effect that no questions will be asked, or that the person producing the dog will be safe from apprehension or inquiry, or that any money paid for its purchase or advanced by way of loan on it will be repaid. The offence will be committed by the printer and publisher of the advertisement as well as by the advertiser himself.

Chapter 2

SALES OF DOGS

Sales of Animals Generally

The first rule applying to the sale of domestic animals, as it applies to goods, is "caveat emptor", or let the buyer beware. In other words, the buyer must accept the animal as he finds it then and later and have no redress for any defects. But the common law and Acts of Parliament have superimposed on this basic rule a number of measures to give buyers some protection.

There can be included as part of the transaction of selling a condition or warranty about a particular quality of the animal, which it is for the buyer to obtain from the seller for the buyer's protection. As will be described later, certain matters will be covered by statute. In so far as they are not, a buyer should cover himself by condition or warranty for particular qualities or virtues which he wants in the animal. A buyer who is concerned that the animal should be fit for a particular purpose which he wants will have protection by statute if his seller is acting in the course of a business (see item (b) on page 16); if not, he should obtain a condition or warranty to that effect. The health and breeding of the animal may be further aspects to be covered.

Such matters are normally secured by a warranty. The difference in legal consequences between a warranty and a condition is that on a breach of warranty the sale is not invalidated and the buyer is entitled only to sue the seller for the loss thereby suffered; but a breach of condition enables the buyer to repudiate the contract of purchase, which means that he may return the animal and be entitled to have his money back.

15

A buyer should consider which form of protection he needs. Both conditions and warranties are effective if given verbally, but then dispute may follow about which it was and about the terms used. It is therefore safer to have it in writing and signed by the seller.

If a diseased dog is sold without warranty or condition, then, unless the seller was guilty of fraud, the buyer suffers the loss under the caveat emptor principle.

The statutory provisions protecting buyers have in modern times grown to substantial proportions and are sometimes complicated. A consideration of these provisions is outside the scope of this book, except to mention that under the Sale of Goods Act of 1979:

(a) there will be an implied condition that the seller has the right to sell the animal;

(b) if the seller is acting in the course of a business, there will be an implied condition that the animal is reasonably fit for any particular purpose which the buyer makes known to the seller showing that the buyer is relying on the seller's skill or judgment;

(c) there will be an implied warranty that the animal is not subject to any charge or incumbrance not disclosed or known to the buyer before the contract of sale.

The remedies for breach of these implied conditions and this warranty are as described above for express conditions and warranties.

Dogs' Pedigrees

It will be a condition of sale, when a dog is sold with a given pedigree, that the pedigree is truly stated. If it is shown to be false, there will be a breach of condition entitling the buyer to repudiate the contract of purchase and claim his money back.

To sell with a false pedigree at a price reflecting the pedigree if true constitutes the criminal offence of obtaining money by false pretences. In cases of disputes, the trading standards officers of the local council will sometimes be able to help, and the Kennel Club will exceptionally arbitrate if the dog is registered with them.

Pet Shops

The Pet Animals Act of 1951 requires that a person keeping a pet shop must be licensed by the district council (in London, by the City Corporation or the borough council, according to the shop's location). The effect of the definition in the Act of "keeping a pet shop" is that persons selling dogs (or other pets) otherwise than in a shop may need to be licensed.

Such a keeping is defined (but with the two qualifications mentioned below) as the carrying on at premises of any nature (including a private dwelling) of a business of selling animals as pets, and includes the keeping of animals in any such premises with a view to their being sold in the course of such a business, whether by their keeper or any other person. Several ingredients of this definition need to be examined.

"Premises" in general legal terminology includes open land as well as buildings, and it is thought that sales in the open air will be equally subject to the Act. See also page 19.

The meaning of "business" is discussed on page 58, and it is suggested that the principles mentioned there should be applied.

The phrase "selling animals as pets" includes, so far as dogs are concerned, their selling wholly or mainly for domestic purposes. The word "animal" is itself defined in the Act as including any description of vertebrate.

17

The second part of the definition makes it clear that the keeping of animals in one place with the object of their being sold by someone other than their keeper at any place or by their keeper at another place will not escape the Act's provisions; that keeping must be licensed. Following this clarification, a case in 1975 decided that a person keeping animals on premises for short periods (48 hours in that case) for the purpose of exporting them nevertheless was keeping a pet shop within the definition, even though the public did not go to the premises to buy animals.

The foregoing definition of "keeping a pet shop" is qualified in two ways. First, a person is not to be treated as keeping a pet shop **only** because he keeps or sells pedigree animals bred by him or the offspring of an animal kept by him as a pet. A pedigree animal is defined to mean an animal of any description which is by its breeding eligible for registration with a recognised club or society keeping a register of animals of that description.

The second qualification arises as follows. If:

(a) a person carries on a business of selling animals as pets; **and**

(b) that business is carried on in conjunction with a business of breeding pedigree animals (as defined above); **and**

(c) the district council are satisfied that the animals sold in the business were acquired by the person with a view to being used, if suitable, for breeding or show purposes; **and**

(d) those animals are not pedigree animals bred by that person; **and**

(e) after their acquisition those animals were found by that person not to be suitable or required for either of the uses described at (c) above;

the district council may direct that the person shall not be

18

treated as keeping a pet shop **by reason only** of his business of selling animals as pets. A pet seller who believes that he should be exempt from licensing on this account should apply to the council for a direction in these terms.

The rules about the licensing of pet shops are similar to those for boarding kennels, for which see pages 58 to 59. The licensing fee, the right of appeal, the duration of the licence and the powers to inspect premises are the same, and corresponding offences are created. The Pet Animals Act 1951 enables the council to attach a condition to the licence providing that mammals will not be sold at too early an age, but the Act does not require the pet shop proprietor to keep a register. Similarly, too, a person convicted of offences under the Act, or under the Protection of Animals Acts (for which, generally, see Chapter 13), may be disqualified by the court from having a pet shop licence and may have any licence held by him cancelled.

Illegal Sales of Dogs

It is an offence for a person who collects or deals in rags, old clothes or similar articles, or for anyone assisting him or acting on his behalf, to sell or deliver, gratuitously or not, to a child under 14 years of age any dog (or other animal):

(a) in or from any shop or other premises (which will mean lands and any other buildings) used for or in connection with the business of a dealer in the articles describe above; or

(b) while engaged in collecting such articles (Public Health (Control of Disease) Act 1984).

Under the Pet Animals Act of 1951 it is an offence to carry on a business of selling animals as pets in any part of a street or public place, or at a stall or barrow in a market.

It is also an offence, whether or not the vendor is operating such a business, to sell an animal as a pet to a person whom the seller has reasonable cause to believe to be under the age of 12. The definitions of "animals" and "selling animals as pets" given on page 17 apply.

Chapter 3

Owners' Responsibilities Under Strict Liability and Negligence Rules

As will be seen from later Chapters, there are many legal rules made, some by Acts of Parliament and some by case law, which govern people's responsibilities for various acts of dogs. These rules relate specifically to dogs. There are also rules framed in wider terms which apply to animals generally, and hence their application to dogs needs to be mentioned here. The rules are found under two headings: strict liability and negligence.

The position under strict liability is regulated by the Animals Act of 1971 and is, unfortunately, complicated. In outline, the Act says that a **keeper** of a dog will be **strictly liable** for **damage** caused by the dog **in certain circumstances** but **will be excused liability** in particular cases. We have to look at each of the emphasised parts of this summary in turn.

A **keeper** of a dog has a special definition which is given in full and discussed on page 32.

"**Strictly liable**" means simply that a dog's keeper will be liable if the dog causes damage, whatever the circumstances; negligence on his part does not have to be proved.

The meaning of "**damage**" is defined to **include** the death of, or injury to, any person, and that in turn includes any disease or any impairment of physical or mental condition. The result of using this definition is not entirely

21

clear, but appears to be that damage to inanimate objects will be within its scope but injury to other animals will not.

The **circumstances** in which there will be liability, unless one of the excuses mentioned below applies, are as follows:

(a) the damage is of a kind which the dog, unless restrained, was likely to cause or which, if caused by the dog, was likely to be severe; **and**

(b) the likelihood of the damage or of its being severe was due to characteristics of the dog not normally found in dogs or not normally so found except at particular times or in particular circumstances; **and**

(c) those characteristics were known to the dog's keeper or were at any time known to a person who at that time had charge of the dog as the keeper's servant or, where the keeper is the head of a household, were known to another keeper of the dog who is a member of that household and under the age of 16.

This is the complicated part of this piece of law. A High Court Judge, no less, once confessed that he had struggled for a considerable time to ascertain its meaning through its remarkably opaque language! Much will depend in each case on the view which the court takes about the characteristics of dogs. In one case it was decided that a propensity to attack people carrying bags is not a normal characteristic of dogs.

The circumstances in which the keeper of a dog **will be excused liability** for damage which it causes are:

(a) Where the damage was due wholly to the fault of the person suffering it; **or**

(b) if the person injured voluntarily accepted the risk of injury, but the employee of a dog's keeper who incurs a risk incidental to his employment is not to be treated as accepting the risk voluntarily; **or**

(c) if the damage was caused by a dog kept at any place to a trespasser there if it is proved:

    (i) **either** that the dog was not kept there for the protection of persons or property;

    (ii) **or**, if the dog was kept there for that purpose, that the keeping for the purpose was not unreasonable.

What is reasonable in case (ii) will depend upon the circumstances; in an old court case it was decided (not surprisingly!) that the keeping of a fierce dog in the access to a house which injured innocent visitors on lawful business was not excusable. See also page 41.

The negligence rules, too, are imprecise. They are based on common law, that is, the decisions of the courts through the years. Liability depends on the person seeking redress being able to satisfy the court that the person whose dog caused the injury or damage owed him a duty to take care, that he failed in that, and that the injury or damage was the result.

The difficulty in this area is being able to establish that duty. Case law is not very helpful, though it does indicate that there is a duty to keep a dog under reasonable control on a public road; this is reinforced by statute – see pages 26 to 27. It may well be that a failure of control in other situations could lead to liability. Clearly, reasonable control of a dog at all times is advisable to prevent accidents and ensuing claims.

Under the negligence rules the person liable will generally be the person having control of the dog at the time of injury or damage; but an owner, even when not such a person, may also be liable in some circumstances.

Claims under the two heads of strict liability and negligence are not mutually exclusive, and may be made in the alternative.

Chapter 4

Dogs and Diseases

If your dog has an infectious or contagious disease, you will be responsible for any damage or injury caused by the disease in the following cases:

(a) If, when you know it to be diseased, you allow it to mingle with other persons' animals.

(b) If, when you know it to be diseased and infectious to persons handling it, you employ a person to handle its carcass who is ignorant of the state of the dog, and that person becomes infected.

(c) If, when you know it to be diseased, you leave the dog with another person for an agreed purpose, knowing that he probably will or may place it with healthy animals, and do not warn that person of the dog's disease.

(d) If you sell the dog with a warranty that it is free from disease, whether you know of the disease or not.

(e) If you are guilty of fraud or concealment about its disease when selling it.

(f) If, knowing the dog to be diseased and that it may be put in with healthy animals, you sell it at public market, fair or auction or, possibly, in a private sale.

A further provision about the sale of diseased dogs may be found on page 16.

It is perhaps worth mentioning here the very strict provisions which would apply if, unfortunately, there were to be an outbreak of rabies in this country.

If you know or suspect that your dog is affected with rabies, or was so affected at its death,–

(a) you must with all practicable speed give written notice of the fact to a diseases of animals inspector of the Ministry of Agriculture or local authority or to the police, unless you reasonably believe that someone else has done so; and

(b) you must, as far as practicable, keep the dog or its carcase separated from other animals.

Government veterinary inspectors are given very wide powers of action if rabies is suspected. They may enter any premises to make enquiries, to examine animals and their carcases, to take samples for diagnosis, and to remove (for veterinary observation or diagnostic tests) animals which are affected with rabies or suspected of infection or which have been in contact with affected or suspected animals. Such animals may be slaughtered by Ministry officials; compensation is payable.

Those involved with animals in these circumstances, e.g., the occupier of the premises where the animals are and those having charge of them, must give information and reasonable assistance to the veterinary inspectors.

The controls on the import of dogs aimed at preventing the introduction of rabies into this country are described in Chapter 16.

Chapter 5

DOGS ON THE ROAD

Straying on to the Road

The Animals Act of 1971 provides that owners of animals and those having control of them have a duty to take reasonable care to see that injury or damage is not caused by their animals straying on to the road. The term "reasonable care" is commonly used in legal parlance to indicate a standard which is flexible enough to take account of varying circumstances. It is not an absolute or strict standard, as with the strict liability provisions mentioned on page 21, but nevertheless demands a fairly high degree of care. The point arose in a case decided in 1981 when the court gave its opinion that if a fence, though not 100% secure, is reasonably adequate to prevent escape, the duty to take reasonable care is fulfilled.

This duty does not automatically demand fencing or other means of containment against the road, but this is generally advisable when a dog is customarily let loose, and is strongly advised if the road is heavily trafficked. On the other hand, if a dog can be trained well enough to keep itself within bounds, no fencing is needed. Responsibility in each case will be determined by the total circumstances of that case.

The duty is only operative in cases of highways (for the meaning of which see page 47), and therefore does not apply to private roads and other private ways.

Clearly, the most serious consequences which could ensue when you are in breach of this duty and your dog causes damage or injury is a motor vehicle accident with ensuing death or injury or a heavy claim for repairs, or all of these. But there will be responsibility also for such lesser incidents as cycle accidents and the knocking over of pedestrians.

Reporting Accidents Involving Dogs

The Road Traffic Act 1988 has laid down rules for conduct when a dog (and certain other animals) is injured in an accident with a motor vehicle on a public road or other road to which the public has access. The rules do not apply when: the dog is in a vehicle or trailer drawn by it; or the vehicle is not intended or adapted for use on roads or is one which can only be used for cutting grass and is controlled by a pedestrian.

The driver of the vehicle must stop. A person having "reasonable grounds" for doing so may ask the driver to supply the name and address of the driver and, if he is not the owner, of the owner of the vehicle, and the vehicle's registration number; the driver must give this information. The "reasonable grounds" are not specified. Clearly, the dog's owner has such grounds and, it is suggested, any person controlling the dog at the time and any member of the owner's family.

The driver should stop for such length of time as in the circumstances will enable any person entitled to do so to require the information from the driver personally. If no one does that, or if for any other reason the driver does not give his name and address, the driver must report the accident to the police as soon as reasonably practicable, and in any case within 24 hours of the accident.

Failure to do any of the things required of him renders the driver liable to prosecution. But (assuming the magistrates believe him) no offence is committed if the driver is unaware of the accident and does not stop.

When a Lead is Necessary

A local authority may by order designate particular roads the effect of which is that it becomes an offence for a person to cause or permit a dog to be on a designated road without it being held on a lead. This is not to apply to dogs proved to be kept for driving or tending sheep or cattle in the course of a trade or business, or proved to be at the time in use under proper control for sporting purposes.

The local authorities which have these powers are, in London, the City Corporation and the London borough councils and, elsewhere, county councils and metropolitan district councils. If they are proposing to make an order, it must be advertised in the local press so that the public may have an opportunity to comment and object, and a public inquiry may be held.

When an order is made, signs giving information about its effect are to be erected in the roads concerned.

Fouling Footways and Other Public Open Spaces

District councils (in London, the City Corporation or a borough council) are enabled to make byelaws about this. There is no set form of byelaw and its wording may vary from place to place, but the following format is commonly found.

The byelaw will make it an offence for a person in charge of a dog to allow it to foul the footway of any street or public place by deposit of its excrement. It is usually provided that it will be a defence if that person satisfies the court that the fouling was not due to culpable neglect or default on his part; and the byelaw may go on to say that the owner of the dog shall be deemed to be in charge of it unless the court is satisfied that at the time of fouling the dog was in the charge of another person. Offences are prosecuted before the magistrates.

The word "street" in this context is likely, through definitions in the byelaw or by reference to definitions elsewhere, to have a wide meaning so as to include any public road or way. And "footway" will usually be interpreted to mean the footpath at the side of a road or public place exclusive of grass verges.

Notices warning of the byelaw should be displayed in the places where the byelaw operates.

Under environmental protection legislation it is made an offence for a dog to foul many kinds of public open spaces unless consent is given by the person controlling the land.

Motorway Rules

The Motorways Traffic (England and Wales) Regulations 1982 contain rules about the handling of all kinds of animals which are carried in a vehicle using a motorway ("vehicle" will include a trailer). To disobey the rules is a criminal offence. The Regulations say that the person in charge of the animal shall so far as practicable secure that:

(a) the animal is not removed from or permitted to leave the vehicle while the vehicle is on the motorway; and

(b) if it escapes from, or it is necessary for it to be removed from or permitted to leave, the vehicle:

  (i) it shall not go or remain on any part of the motorway except the verge, which is defined to mean any part of the road other than a carriageway or central reservation, and

  (ii) while it is not on or in the vehicle, it must be held on a lead or otherwise kept under proper control.

29

But the person in charge of the animal need not comply with these requirements if so directed by the police or if such is indicated by a traffic sign.

Chapter 6

TRESPASSING DOGS

A dog may be said to be trespassing when it is on property where it has no right to be or, more correctly, where its owner has no right or permission to allow it to be. The law is fairly precise about liability for certain kinds of trespass by a dog, but is not so clear in other instances.

If a dog of its own accord enters land without permission but does no more, its owner is not liable under civil law for the trespass; nor is it any criminal offence.

Nineteenth Century cases have decided that a dog's owner is liable under civil law if he deliberately sends his dog on to somebody else's land in pursuit of game (no entry on the land by the owner being necessary), or if he allows the dog to roam at large knowing it to be addicted to destroying game. It is not clear what the consequences are if the dog is so sent for another purpose; possibly the owner would be liable for damage thereby caused.

Special rules operate when a trespassing dog kills or injures livestock, and these will be considered in a moment. There then remains the situation in which the dog of its own accord trespasses and causes damage otherwise than to livestock. Again, the law is not clear, but probably the position is that the dog's owner will be liable for any damage which it is in the nature of a dog to commit.

Cases of dogs worrying livestock are governed by two statutes: the Animals Act of 1971 deals with civil liability; and the Dogs (Protection of Livestock) Act 1953 regulates criminal responsibility. Liability under one head does not of course exclude liability under the other.

Except as noted below, the keeper of a dog is liable for the damage it causes by killing or injuring livestock. Three parts of this statement need individual examination.

The 1971 Act gives a special meaning to the word "keeper". A person is a keeper of a dog if he either owns it, or has it in his possession, or is the head of a household of which a member under 16 years old owns the dog or possesses it. Such a person remains the keeper of the dog until someone else fulfilling these qualifications succeeds him as keeper. But a person who takes possession of a dog to prevent it causing damage or to restore it to its owner does not, just because of that possession, become its keeper.

Despite all this detail, some imprecision remains about the identify of the head of a household. Probably, and despite modern trends, in the common case of a household with husband, wife and children the husband is assumed to be its head. But proof of the fact could be difficult, and establishing the identify of the head in many households of different composition more so.

Cases decided prior to the Act indicate that injury in this context may include indirect injury. For example, foals injuring themselves as the result of a dog barking at them, and poultry ceasing to lay as a result of shock following a dog's presence.

The 1971 Act has a long definition of "livestock". It means all of the following:

(a) Cattle, horses, asses, mules, hinnies (which are the off-spring of she-asses by stallions), sheep, pigs, goats, and deer not in a wild state.

(b) The domestic varieties of fowls, turkeys, ducks, geese, guinea-fowls, pigeons, peacocks and quails.

(c) While in captivity only, pheasants, partridges and grouse.

Liability is avoided in the cases listed below. But otherwise it matters not what active or passive role is played by the dog's keeper (as defined). It is enough that he is its keeper and the dog does the damage. There is no liability:

(1) if the damage to the livestock is due wholly to the fault of the person whose livestock it is; **or**

(2) if the livestock was killed or injured on land on to which it had strayed **and**:

    (i) **either** the dog belonged to the occupier of that land, **or**

    (ii) its presence on that land was authorised by him.

Where damage is caused by two or more dogs acting together, the law regards each dog as causing the whole of the damage, and consequently the keeper of each can be held responsible for the whole damage.

Under the Dogs (Protection of Livestock) Act 1953, if a dog worries livestock on agricultural land, its owner and, if it is in the charge of anyone else, that person also, is guilty of an offence and can be prosecuted and fined, unless one of the defences later mentioned can be established. Here, again, there are definitions of a number of the terms used.

"Livestock" are: bulls, cows, oxen, heifers, calves, sheep, goats, swine, horses, asses, mules, and domestic fowls, turkeys, geese and ducks.

"Agricultural land" means land used as arable, meadow or grazing land, or for the purposes of poultry or pig farming, market gardens, allotments, nursery grounds or orchards; and, it has been decided, a cricket field on which sheep are grazing will come within this definition.

There is a long definition of what worrying livestock (as that word is already defined) means. It is:

(a) attacking livestock; **or**

(b) chasing them (which will include running among them so as to alarm them) in such a way as may be reasonably expected to cause them injury (which here has the same meaning as described on page 32) or suffering or, in the case of females, abortion or loss or diminution in their produce; **or**

(c) being at large (i.e., not on a lead or otherwise under close control) in a field or enclosure in which there are sheep.

But case (c) does **not** apply to the following dogs:

(i) a dog owned by, or in the charge of, the occupier of the field or enclosure, the owner of the sheep or a person authorised by that occupier or owner. (This authorisation appears to mean authority or permission given to the person to have his dog in the field or enclosure. The authority is not required to be in writing, but ideally it should be to safeguard the authorised persons's position if he were to be prosecuted);

(ii) police dogs, guide dogs, trained sheep dogs, working gun dogs, and packs of hounds.

The offence of worrying livestock will not be committed (and the defendant therefore is entitled to be acquitted) in either of the following cases:

(A) if, being the owner of the dog, he satisfies the court that at the time in question the dog was in the charge of some other person whom he reasonably believed to be a fit and proper person to be in charge of it;

(B) if, being the owner of the dog or in charge of it, he satisfies the court that at the material time the livestock were trespassing on the land in question and the dog was owned by, or in the charge of, the occupier of that

34

land or a person authorised by that owner or occupier. (As to "authorise", see paragraph (i) above.) But this will not be a defence if the authorised person causes the dog to attack the livestock.

The police may intervene in some cases of dogs worrying livestock. If a police officer reasonably believes that a dog found on what appears to him to be agricultural land has been worrying livestock there, and no person is present who admits to being its owner or in charge of it, the officer may, in order to find out the owner, seize and keep the dog until the owner has claimed it and paid the expenses of detention. (The same definitions for "livestock" and "agricultural land" as are given on page 33 apply in this situation). The procedure to be operated by the police after seizure is that used when a stray dog is detained, for which see pages 48 to 49.

For the occasions when the killing or injuring of a dog which is attacking animals or human beings is justified, see Chapter 10.

Chapter 7

Nuisances, Byelaws and Hygiene Regulations

Nuisances

The keeping of any animals in such a position or in such circumstances as to cause a substantial discomfort or annoyance to the public in general or to a particular person constitutes in law the civil wrong of nuisance. The remedy is by action in the courts claiming, as appropriate, an award of damages and/or an injunction; the latter is an order of the court forbidding the continuance of the nuisance on penalty of a fine or imprisonment.

Dogs may cause discomfort or annoyance, for example, by excessive barking, especially if late at night, or by a number of them running loose. But the effect must be substantial, and it is always a question of degree whether a particular activity in given circumstances constitutes a nuisance; some inconveniences have to be tolerated.

In addition to nuisances at common law which have just been described, Acts of Parliament have created what are known as statutory nuisances. Amongst other things, it is a statutory nuisance to keep any animal in such a place or manner as to be injurious to, or likely to cause injury to, health, or to be a nuisance. It appears that what is meant by being a nuisance in this context is carrying on an activity affecting public health, though not necessarily causing injury to health or annoyance to any particular person or injury to any particular property.

There is a statutory procedure which is operated by district councils for dealing with these nuisances. It involves: the service of an abatement notice and, if that is not heeded, a summons to, and an order by, the magistrates' court; fines for non-compliance; abatement by the council; and recovery of the council's costs of abatement and legal costs.

Basically, common law and statutory nuisances are concerned with the same thing, the causing of substantial discomfort or annoyance to people. The latter type of nuisance is generally more concerned with public health considerations, whilst the common law is more likely to be called in aid to settle private disputes.

Byelaws

Byelaws are a kind of subordinate legislation which may be made by a variety of organisations and for many different purposes and situations. Some byelaws affect dogs and the following are the most common instances of these.

District councils, under their powers to make byelaws for good rule and government and the suppression of nuisances, will often have a byelaw in force dealing with noisy animals; this may be used for complaints about barking dogs. Its terms will commonly provide that a person must not keep in any house, building or premises any noisy animal which causes a serious nuisance to residents in the neighbourhood. But there will be no prosecution for this unless the nuisance continues after a fortnight has elapsed from the date on which a notice alleging a nuisance is served on the person keeping the animal. The notice must be signed by at least three householders living within hearing of the animal.

Enquiries can be made at the district council offices to find out whether such a byelaw exists and, if so, its precise terms. (In London the council concerned is the borough council, or the City Corporation in the City of London.) These councils are required to have their byelaws available for free inspection and to supply copies on payment.

Breach of the byelaw may result in the offending person being prosecuted in the magistrates' court. The penalty is likely to be a moderate fine, but the byelaw may provide for a further small fine for each day on which the nuisance continues after conviction.

Many organisations controlling public open spaces have byelaws; the details are sometimes accessible on site, but in other cases enquiries must be made. Byelaws may be made for national parks, areas of outstanding natural beauty, National Trust property, nature reserves, common land, large forest areas, and land and waterways to which the public have access by agreement or order.

The Forestry Commission Byelaws of 1982 operate on Forestry Commission land to which the public have access. So far as dogs may be concerned, these provide that a person shall not, except with the Commissioners' written authority:

(a) permit any animal in the person's charge to be out of control;

(b) permit a dog for which the person is responsible to disturb, worry or chase any bird or animal or, on being requested by an officer of the Commissioners to do so, fail to keep the dog on a leash;

(c) intentionally disturb, injure, catch, destroy or take any bird, fish, reptile or animal, or attempt to do so;

(d) intentionally disturb, damage or destroy the burrow, den, set or lair of any wild animal.

Water authorities and internal drainage boards may make byelaws applying to reservoirs, waterways, other inland waters and land under their control. These may deal with such matters as:

(a) prohibiting the washing of animals in the water. (The British Waterways Board have a similar byelaw relating to their canals – except the Gloucester and Sharpness Canal.)

(b) prohibiting the destruction, injury or disturbance of wild animals.

(c) ordering dog owners and others in charge of them to keep them under proper control and to restrain them from causing annoyance to other people, from worrying other animals or water fowl and from entering the water.

The British Railways Board's byelaws of 1971 have several provisions affecting animals generally. These include: the power to exclude animals causing or likely to cause annoyance or damage; the exclusion of animals from moving platforms; and directions about where animals may be left or placed.

Hygiene Regulations

Under the Food Hygiene (General) Regulations 1970 a business or undertaking, whether run for profit or not, in which food is sold or supplied for human consumption is required to observe a number of hygiene regulations. These include rules designed to prevent dogs and other live animals from coming into contact with food.

Shops serving food and their customers are exhorted by the public health authorities to exclude dogs from the shops, but guide dogs for the blind are permitted entry.

Chapter 8

DANGEROUS AND FEROCIOUS DOGS

Dangerous Dogs

Until 1991 the only Act of Parliament which provided court procedures for dealing with dangerous dogs as such was the Dogs Act of 1871. Following a series of attacks on people by the more vicious kinds of dogs, a Dangerous Dogs Act was passed in the summer of 1991; this provided better means for dealing with such dogs. First, however, we look at the provisions of the 1871 Act.

Dogs Act 1871

Under this Act a complaint may be made to a magistrates' court that a dog is dangerous and not kept under proper control. If the magistrates find that the dog is dangerous, they may either order the dog's owner to keep it under proper control or order it to be destroyed. A fine can be imposed for breach of either kind of order.

The main defects of this procedure have now been remedied by the Dangerous Dogs Act of 1991. Previously, there was doubt about when a dog could be said to be dangerous. If a dog was proved to have injured cattle or poultry, or to have chased sheep, an order under the 1871 Act could be made. Whilst attacks on people would generally justify an order, the position was uncertain in the case of incidents involving other kinds of animals.

Now, magistrates may make an order without proof that any person had been injured. Injuring cattle or poultry still provides justification for an order. It appears that the resultant position is that magistrates now have a wide discretion and may make an order in any circumstances where they find a dog to be dangerous.

Before 1991, magistrates could not elaborate on the means of control when making a proper control order. Today, their order may specify those means; muzzling, keeping on a lead, exclusion from named places and any other measures of control are permitted. Also, if magistrates believe that neutering of a male dog would make it less dangerous, they may order that to be done.

The need for proper control is not limited to public places, but extends, it has been decided, to places where the dog is on the owner's private property to which other people have a right of access.

A control order or a destruction order may be made even though the owner did not know that his dog was dangerous. Though normally a control order will first be made, magistrates would not be acting improperly solely because they made a destruction order in the first instance.

The police are the proper people in the majority of cases to start proceedings in the magistrates' court, but others may do so. An appeal may be made to the Crown Court against a destruction order or a control order.

A person who sets his dog on another person who is wounded by the dog will be guilty of the offence of malicious wounding under the Offences Against the Persons Act 1861.

Dangerous Dogs Act 1991

This Act tackles the problem of dangerous dogs in four new ways:

(1) By prohibiting possession of named breeds except under strictly controlled conditions.

(2) By authorising the imposition of restrictions on other dogs believed to be a serious danger to the public.

(3) By imposing sanctions on the owners of dogs and those in charge of them which are dangerously out of control in a public place.

(4) By imposing sanctions on the owners of dogs and those in charge of them who allow them to injure persons on private property.

(1) Four types of dog are named by, or under powers in, the 1991 Act. These are: the pit bull terrier; the Japanese tosa; the Dogo Argentino and the Fila Braziliero.

By Government order, other dogs of a type appearing to be bred for fighting or to have the characteristics of such a type may be added to this list.

From 12th August 1991, it is an offence: to breed or breed from any such dog; to sell, exchange, or to offer, advertise or expose it for sale or exchange; to make, or offer to make, a gift of it, or advertise or expose it as a gift; to allow it to be in a public place without being muzzled or kept on a lead; or to abandon it or allow it to stray.

From 30th November 1991, it is an offence for a person to have possession or custody of any of the listed dogs unless the following requirements are met. These are, briefly, that particulars of the dog be reported to the police, that the dog be neutered and carry identification of neutering, that third party insurance cover be provided, and that a certificate of exemption shall be in force and its requirements complied with. The Index of Exempted Dogs has been appointed as agent by the Home Office to manage these exemption arrangements and the compensation scheme mentioned below.

Owners of dogs who have arranged for them to be destroyed before 30th November 1991 will receive compensation for their loss provided the prescribed conditions are met. Compensation is settled at £25 for pit bull terriers, £100 for other banned breeds and £25 for the cost of destruction in either case.

In practice, these measures are aimed at the pit bull terrier, the other named breeds being very rare in this country. On the face of it, the measures would appear to be sufficiently drastic to deal with the situation. The problem arises in determining whether or not a dog is a pit bull terrier. The Act's definition is "any dog of the type known as the pit bull terrier", and it provides that in any prosecution it is to be presumed that the dog is a pit bull terrier unless the accused brings sufficient evidence to the contrary. Several early prosecutions under the Act have failed because the defendant has been able to convince the court, through the evidence of an expert witness, that his dog was not a pit bull terrier but a dog of a similar appearance, such as a Staffordshire bull terrier, a Labrador cross or other cross-breed which cannot rightly be called a pit bull terrier.

The true pit bull terrier is itself a cross-breed; but canine purists and the Home Office (who are responsible for the legislation) disagree about the breeds from which it is bred. No wonder confusion ensues! The remedy will not be easy to find.

(2) Distinct arrangements are made under the 1991 Act for types of dog which, though not partly banned as described, are seen by the Government to present a serious danger to the public. These arrangements, which are yet to be brought into force by Government

order, will nominate types of dogs of this description and impose restrictions on them. The restrictions, breach of which may lead to prosecution, fines and imprisonment, can only include banning the dogs from public places without being muzzled or kept on a lead, and prohibiting their abandonment or straying.

(3) An offence is committed by the owner of a dog, **and** by any other person in charge of it at the time, if the dog is dangerously out of control in a public place. A more serious offence will be committed if the dog, while so out of control, injures a person.

The owner of a dog, who was not in charge of it at the time, will have a defence if he proves that the dog was then in the charge of somebody whom he reasonably believed to be a fit and proper person to be in charge of it.

Where the dog is owned by a person less than 16 years old, the owner, for the purpose of this offence, will include the head of the household, if any, of which that person is a member.

(4) An offence is committed by the owner of a dog who allows it to enter a place which is not a public place and, while it is there, it injures any person or there are grounds for reasonable apprehension that it will do so. If a person other than the owner of the dog is in charge of it at the time, that person, and not the owner, will be liable. The maximum penalties on conviction are more serious if injury occurs.

It will be seen that this offence governs control of dogs on private property, whilst that relating to public places is as described at (3) above.

In addition to imposing fines and imprisonment, a court convicting a person for any of the offences described at (1), (2), (3) and (4) above may order the destruction of the dog involved. The dog **must** be destroyed if the offence concerns one of the partly banned breeds, or if the offence under (3) or (4) involves actual injury. The court **may** also disqualify the offender in cases (1), (3) or (4) above, for as long as it thinks necessary, for having custody of a dog.

Police officers and authorised officers of a local authority are given wide powers to enter and search premises and to seize dogs involved in offences or suspected offences; in some cases a magistrate's warrant is needed.

Ferocious Dogs

Except in the Greater London area, it is an offence, which originates in the Town Police Clauses Act of 1847, for any person in any street: to let an unmuzzled ferocious dog be at large so that it obstructs or annoys the residents or passengers in the street or puts them in danger; or to set on or urge any dog to attack, worry or put in fear any person or animal. The word "street" here is given an extended meaning to include any road, square, court, alley, thoroughfare or public passage.

The courts have not pronounced on the meaning to be given to "ferocious", but a dog may be regarded as ferocious if it appears to be untamed and certainly if it is shown to have unusually vicious tendencies. In adjudicating in any prosecution the magistrates will form a view based on the behaviour of the dog at the time and on any evidence given about its previous conduct. Less extreme behaviour may make the dog liable to be dealt with as a dangerous dog, for which see the preceding pages.

Clearly, a dog will not be at large when it is held on a

lead. It may be argued, since "at large" means at liberty or free, that an unleashed dog answering obediently to the commands of the person in charge of it is also not at large; though in that situation the dog should not be annoying or endangering people or other animals, but may be obstructing people. If a dog may exhibit tendencies in a street which might be described as ferocious, it is sensible (if it has to be there) for it to be muzzled when, whatever its behaviour, the offence of letting it be at large cannot be committed.

In the Metropolitan Police District a similar offence has been created by the Metropolitan Police Act of 1839. This differs only from the first part of the 1847 Act offence in that it is sufficient that an unmuzzled dog be at large (no obstruction, annoyance or danger need be shown), and that the place of the offence is described as any thoroughfare or public place.

Chapter 9

Dog Collars and Stray Dogs

Dog Collars

Under the Control of Dogs Order of 1992 every dog, while in a highway or place of public resort, must wear a collar with the name and address of its owner inscribed on it or on a plate or badge attached to it.

A highway is a road or other way over which the public have the right to pass to and fro; it need not necessarily be maintained by a highway authority. A place of public resort has been said to mean a place to which the public goes as a matter of fact, as distinct from a matter of right, and notwithstanding that a charge is made for admission.

But a dog collar is not needed for:

(a) a pack of hounds; or

(b) any dog while being used for sporting purposes, for the capture or destruction of vermin, or for the driving or tending of cattle or sheep; or

(c) any dog while being used on official duties by the Armed Forces, Customs and Excise officers or the police; or

(d) any dog while being used in emergency rescue work; or

(e) any dog registered with the Guide Dogs for the Blind Association.

If a collar is not worn when required, the dog may be seized by the police and treated by them as a stray, for which see the heading "Stray Dogs" below. Also, its owner and any person in charge of it causing or permitting the dog to be in a highway or place of public resort are each guilty of an offence and may be prosecuted and fined, unless they had lawful authority or excuse.

It is unlikely that an ordinary defendant could plead lawful authority as a defence; that would however bar the conviction of a policeman during the course of seizing the dog. The other defence – having a lawful excuse – could be available, for example, to an owner who was prosecuted and who was able to satisfy the magistrates that he was neither in charge of the dog at the time nor had any part in allowing it to be in a highway or place of public resort; and, further, that he honestly but mistakenly believed on reasonable grounds that the dog was to be used by another person for one of the purposes described in item (b) above.

Stray Dogs

(1) Seizure by the police

The Dogs Act of 1906 enables a police officer to seize any dog found in a highway or place of public resort (for the meanings of these terms, see page 47) which he has reason to believe is a stray. A dog found on any other land or premises may be similarly seized if the owner or occupier consents. The officer seizing the dog may then detain it until the owner has claimed it and paid all expenses incurred in its detention.

If the dog is wearing a collar showing an address, or the owner is otherwise known, the officer must serve on the person whose address is given or the known owner (as the case may be) written notice that the dog has been seized and is liable to be sold or destroyed if not claimed within 7 clear days after service of the notice.

After 7 days from service of the notice, or from original

detention of the dog if the police have not been able to serve a notice, if the owner has not claimed it and paid the expenses of its detention, the detaining officer may sell the dog or have it destroyed. But it must not be given or sold for purposes of vivisection and, if destroyed, that must be done so as to cause as little pain as possible.

The police must keep a register of all dogs seized by them and record their particulars. It is open for public inspection at all reasonable times for a fee of 5p.

(2) Finding by a private person

The finder of a stray dog must at once either return it to its owner or take it to the nearest police station or to the dog warden of the local authority for the area, advising them where it was found.

If the finder takes the dog to the police, he may choose to keep it and, having supplied his particulars to the police, will be allowed to do so. He must however keep the dog for at least one month; failure to do so is an offence for which he can be prosecuted and fined. If the finder chooses not to keep the dog, the police will treat it as if it had been seized by them as a stray, for which see 'Seizure by the police' above.

If the finder takes the dog to the local authority's dog warden, the ensuing procedure is more involved. The finder may again choose to keep the dog or not. If he decides to keep it, the following steps are taken:

(a) the finder supplies his particulars to the dog warden;

(b) the dog warden also records a description of the dog, any information on the dog's collar, and particulars about its finding;

(c) where the dog's owner can be identified and readily contacted, the dog warden will try to contact him and give him an opportunity to collect the dog;

49

(d) failing collection by the owner, the finder will be allowed to keep the dog if the dog warden's enquiries about his suitability as a dog owner are satisfactory;

(e) the dog warden warns the finder of his obligation to keep the dog for at least one month (if unclaimed by the owner) on pain of prosecution.

If the finder of a stray, having taken it to the dog warden, tells him that he does not want to keep it, the dog warden will retain the dog and, unless he believes that it is not a stray, will treat it as a dog seized by him, for which see 'Seizure by dog wardens' below.

(3) Seizure by dog wardens

From 1st April 1992, each district council is to appoint a dog warden. It is his duty to seize (if practicable) any dog which he believes to be a stray and to detain it. Where it is found on private property, he must have the prior consent of the owner or occupier.

The dog warden must then serve notice on the dog's owner if he can be identified. This notice will be similar to that served by the police, for which see page 48. If the owner claims the dog, he must pay a prescribed sum of £25 and the expenses of its detention by the dog warden before he can collect it.

If not claimed within 7 days of seizure or, if a notice has been served, within 7 days of its service, the dog warden may sell or give the dog to a suitable person or to a dogs' home (who in either case will become its owner), or may have it destroyed. It is not to be disposed of for vivisection.

The dog warden is obliged to keep a register of dogs seized. This will include a description of each dog, any information on its collar, particulars of its finding and of any 7-day notice served, and details of the dog's disposal or of its return to its owner. The register will be available for free inspection by the public.

The wisdom of ensuring that your dog at all times wears a collar and carries the required particulars is evident. Otherwise, within 7 days of being collected as a stray it can be destroyed or handed over to another person from whom you may have no right to reclaim it, and you may not be aware that this is happening. Obviously, if your dog strays and is lost, you should urgently make enquiries of all local police stations and the local authority's dog warden.

Chapter 10

THE RULES ABOUT KILLING AND INJURING DOGS

The Civil Law

If his dog is wrongfully killed or injured by another person, the dog's owner will be able to sue that person and recover damages for his loss. The law says that there are three situations in which a killing or injury is not wrongful, and it is only in those situations that the owner will have no claim.

The first of these situations, which is regulated by the Animals Act of 1971 and is rather complicated, is when a person (called below "the killer") kills or injures another dog to protect livestock. The meaning of "livestock" is as given on page 32. The killer will be excused liability if he fulfils all of the following conditions:

(1) he was acting for the protection of livestock;

(2) he was entitled to act for the protection of livestock;

(3) within 48 hours of the killing or injury he gave notice of it to the officer in charge of a police station.

The 1971 Act goes on to lay down more precisely when a killer shall be treated as acting for the protection of livestock and when he shall be treated as entitled so to act. So, to fulfil condition (1):

(a) **either** the dog must have been worrying or about to worry livestock and there were no other reasonable means of ending or preventing the worrying;

(b) **or** the dog had been worrying livestock, had not left the

52

vicinity and was not under the control of any person, and there were no practicable means of ascertaining to whom it belonged.

And, to fulfil condition (2):

(i) the livestock, or the land on which it was at the time of killing, must belong to the killer or to some other person under whose express or implied authority the killer was acting; **but**

(ii) the situation must **not** be one in which the livestock was killed or injured on land on to which it had strayed **and** the dog belonged to the occupier of that land or its presence there was authorised by the occupier. (In these circumstances the 1971 Act provides that the dog's keeper shall not be liable for damage to the livestock; see item (2) on page 33.)

The following points of detail arise on the foregoing.

Written notice to the police is not mandatory but is advisable for the killer's protection in the case of later proceedings against him. He should have a copy of the notice receipted by the police officer and endorsed by the officer with the time and date of receipt.

The 1971 Act does not have a definition of "worrying". It is suggested that the definition given on pages 33 and 34 be used as a guide, but omitting part (c) of it as being as too artificial in the present context.

In the case of items (a) and (b) above, the Act states that a belief on reasonable grounds that the conditions described were so will be sufficient. In other words, a killer pleading those conditions will be successful if he can satisfy the court that he believed they were so and had reasonable grounds for that belief, even though others might have taken a different view at the time.

For the purpose if items (i) and (ii) above, an animal

belongs to any person if he owns it or has it in his possession, and land belongs to any person if he is the occupier of it.

The second situation in which the killing or injuring of a dog is justified is when it is done by a human being in self-defence. Presumably there would be justification for a killer so acting in defence of another person being attacked. It is also uncertain whether a killing or injury is justified when the dog is running away after such an attack.

It seems clear that there would have to be some correlation between the severity of the attack and the severity of the counter-measures used. At one extreme, to kill a dog following a nip in the leg would not be justified; and, at the other, a person is not required to fear for his life before hurting the dog.

The third situation arises when a dog attacks domestic animals which are not livestock (as that word is defined on page 32). In this case the killing or injuring of a dog is justified if:

(a) at the material time the dog was actually attacking the animals **or**, if left at large, would renew the attack so that the animals would be left in real and imminent danger unless renewal was prevented; **and**

(b) **either** there was in fact no practicable means other than shooting of stopping the present attack or a renewal of attack, **or** that, having regard to all the circumstances in which he found himself, the killer acted reasonably in regarding the shooting as necessary.

The rules in this third situation derive from case law (as, too, do those in the second situation). There is therefore no such specific protection for a defendant on the grounds of reasonable belief as applies to items (a) and (b) in the first situation – see page 53. A court would assess all the circumstances and evidence, including the reasonableness of the killer's behaviour.

It is doubtful whether there is a defence to a civil claim for killing or injuring another's dog because it is attacking wild animals on one's land; though protective measures for game may be taken – see page 77.

It is not permissible to tempt other people's dogs to destruction by devices on one's own land; the dogs' owners would be entitled to sue for damages. This rule derives from an old law case concerned with traps baited with strong smelling meat.

The Criminal Law

The criminal law is found in the Criminal Damage Act of 1971 which is concerned with the destruction or damage by one person of another person's property. Since domestic animals are capable of ownership (see page 13), the 1971 Act applies to the killing or injuring of dogs and other domestic animals.

An offence is committed if a person without lawful excuse kills or injures a dog belonging to another person intending to do so or being reckless as to whether the dog would be killed or injured. Certain ingredients of this statement need examination.

The 1971 Act sets out the circumstances in which a person shall be treated as having a lawful excuse and in which therefore no offence is committed. This is so, firstly, if at the time of the alleged offence he believed that the person or persons whom he believed to be entitled to consent to the injury or killing had so consented or would have so consented if he or they had known of the injury or killing and its circumstances.

There is also a lawful excuse if the person killed or injured the dog in order to protect property belonging to himself or to another person, or to protect a right or interest in property which was or which he believed to be vested in himself or another person; **and** at the time of the alleged offence he believed that :

(a) the property, right or interest was in immediate need of protection; **and**

(b) the means of protection adopted or proposed were or would have been reasonable having regard to all the circumstances.

In the cases where in the last two paragraphs there are references to the person's beliefs, the Act provides that it is immaterial whether those beliefs were justified, provided they were honestly held.

The Act says that, for the purpose of interpreting the foregoing paragraphs, a dog or other property is to be treated as belonging to any person who has :

(a) the custody or control of it; **or**

(b) any proprietary right or interest in it, but not an interest arising only from an agreement to transfer or grant an interest; **or**

(c) a mortgage of it.

It appears that the word "proprietary" is here used to mean more than simple ownership and might extend to a leasing or hiring of, or a licence to use, property.

As a final comment on the original statement of the offence, it is emphasised that an accidental killing or injuring of a dog, without intention or recklessness in the act, will not be an offence.

The killing or injuring of one's own dog is not by itself an offence, but it would be so if cruelty were used, for which see Chapter 13.

A person convicted of an offence of killing or injuring another's dog may be ordered by a magistrates' court to pay compensation of up to £2000 for any loss or damage resulting from the offence. In many cases therefore it will be unnecessary for an aggrieved dog owner to use the civil law with its attendant expense. It is possible to prosecute the criminal offence privately if the law enforcement authorities do not do so.

D

Chapter 11

BOARDING KENNELS AND BREEDING KENNELS

Boarding Kennels

The Animals Boarding Establishment Act 1963 requires boarding kennels for dogs and cats to be licensed by district councils (in London, by the City Corporation or the borough council according to the kennels' location).

The activity requiring a licence is the keeping of such kennels, and this is defined as the carrying on at any premises (including a private dwelling) of a business of providing accommodation for other people's dogs and cats. But the Act states that a licence is not needed if :

(a) the accommodation is provided in connection with a business of which the provision of boarding accommodation is not the main activity, e.g., a vet who provides board as a sideline to his practice; **or**

(b) if dogs or cats are kept on premises pursuant to a requirement under the diseases of animals legislation.

Also, since this definition incorporates a business element, if the boarding of the animals is not a business, a licence is unnecessary. Whilst the word "business" commonly means an activity carried on for profit, it is not safe to assume, in the light of past court cases considering the meaning in other contexts, that profit is a necessary ingredient. It is suggested that: if boarding is a regular practice, it needs a licence, whether done for profit or not; but if done for friends when on holiday, or in similar helping circumstances, on payment only of the cost of the animals' keep, it does not.

The granting of a licence is at the council's discretion. The 1963 Act requires them to pay particular attention to ensuring that the animals will be suitably accommodated, fed, exercised and protected from disease and fire, and that a proper register is kept showing their dates of arrival and departure and their owners' names and addresses. A licence should contain conditions to these ends, and the council may add other conditions.

A fee for the licence will be charged; there is no maximum. The licence will run, at the applicant's choice, from the day it is granted to the end of the year, or from the beginning of next year to the end of that year.

An applicant aggrieved by the refusal of a licence or by any of the conditions included in a licence granted to him may appeal to a magistrates' court.

Councils may authorise their officers, and vets, to inspect licensed kennels. It is an offence intentionally to obstruct or delay their entry or inspection. It is also an offence to keep kennels without a licence when one is needed, or to fail to comply with a condition of a licence.

As well as imposing any other punishment, a court convicting for these offences (or for a number of other offences under Acts concerned with animals) may cancel the defendant's licence and disqualify him from keeping kennels for as long as it thinks fit. The defendant may appeal against these decisions to the Crown Court.

When the licence holder dies, the licence is treated as having been granted to his personal representatives for 3 months after the death. The council may extend and re-extend the 3 months if satisfied that that is necessary for winding up the deceased's estate and that no other circumstances make it undesirable.

Breeding Kennels

The Breeding of Dogs Act 1973 requires dog breeding kennels to be licensed by district councils (in London, by the City Corporation or the borough council according to the kennels' location).

The activity required to be licensed is the keeping of such kennels, and keeping is defined as the carrying on at premises of any nature (including a private dwelling) of a business of breeding dogs with a view to their being sold in the course of that business, either by their keeper or any other person. Dog breeding kennels are defined as any premises (including a private dwelling) where more than two bitches are kept for the purpose of breeding for sale.

It will be seen that no licence is necessary if only one or two bitches are kept, or if there is no intention to sell the offspring and none is sold however many bitches are kept. In relation to the meaning of "business" (see page 58), there is perhaps slight scope for arguing that a licence is unnecessary when, though more than two bitches are kept, sales are very infrequent.

The rules for the licensing of breeding kennels are so similar to those for boarding kennels (see page 59) as not to merit repetition here. The only significant difference is that a register of animals need not be kept. The fee for the licence is said by the Act to be £2 or such reasonable sum as the council may fix.

Under new legislation, by means of a magistrates' warrant, greater powers of entry to and inspection of breeding kennels have been given to local authority officers and their vets.

Chapter 12

Guard Dogs

Following a number of accidents in which dogs guarding property savaged people, the Guard Dogs Act was passed in 1975 and the following of its provisions are operative.

For the purposes of the Act a guard dog is defined as a dog which is being used to protect premises, or property kept on the premises, or a person guarding the premises or such property. The word "premises" is defined, and two parts of that definition also need explanation.

"Premises" means land (other than agricultural land and land within the curtilage of a dwelling house) and buildings, including parts of buildings other than dwelling houses. "Agricultural land" means land used as arable, meadow or grazing land, or for the purpose of poultry farming, pig farming, market gardens, allotments, nursery grounds or orchards. A curtilage of a dwelling house is its garden and more immediate surrounds. In summary, therefore, the rules about guard dogs which follow apply to all land and buildings except houses, their surrounds and farmland in a wide sense of that word.

The 1975 Act makes it an offence to use, or permit the use of, a guard dog at any premises (as defined above) unless a person (in the Act and here called "the handler") who is capable of controlling the dog is present on the premises, and the dog is under the control of the handler at all times while it is being used as a guard dog, except while it is secured so that it is not at liberty to roam the premises. The handler's duty to control the dog may only be relaxed if another handler capable of controlling it has control of it so that it cannot roam.

A guard dog is not to be used at all unless a notice warning of its presence is clearly shown at each entrance to the premises.

As will have been seen, the foregoing provisions are matters of criminal law and do not themselves provide for compensation for a person attacked by a guard dog. However, the Powers of Criminal Courts Act 1973 empowers a court in any case where a defendant is convicted of an offence to award compensation of up to £2000 to any person for personal injury, loss or damage resulting from that offence. If there is no prosecution (a private prosecution may be undertaken), or if that is unsuccessful, the person attacked must rely on such rights as he has under the civil laws of strict liability and negligence, for which see Chapter 3.

The parts of the 1975 Act which are not yet operative relate to the licensing by district councils of kennels at which guard dogs are kept.

Chapter 13

CRUELTY TO DOGS

Introduction

The foundation of the present legislation on cruelty to animals is still today the Protection of Animals Act of 1911. This has been reinforced over the years by other Acts of Parliament and by statutory regulations made under powers given in those Acts. Some parts of this legislation apply only to dogs, whilst other parts apply to most kinds of domestic animals or to particular kinds of them. (References in this Chapter to dogs in the context of individual offences do not imply that other animals are necessarily excluded.)

The different types of cruelty are covered in the individual sub-headings below. Some of these, as will be seen, are specifically described as offences of cruelty. Where this is the case, readers should refer also to the last sub-heading, "Consequences of Conviction for Offences of Cruelty", to obtain complete information.

In all instances, whether described as offences of cruelty or not, it will be a defence to show that the act complained of was lawfully done under the Animals (Scientific Procedures) Act 1986, i.e., as part of a licensed experiment, for which see page 65.

In cases where an offence is created if an owner permits the act described, the owner is deemed to permit cruelty if he fails to exercise reasonable care and supervision in protecting his dog from it.

There are many other protective laws which serve to eliminate or reduce the suffering of animals. So far as they affect dogs, such laws are dealt with in the section of Chapter 2 on pet shops, Chapter 4 (diseased dogs), Chapter 10 about the killing and injuring of dogs, Chapter 11 (boarding and breeding kennels), and Chapter 14 on performing dogs.

Abandonment

Any person, being the owner or having charge or control of a dog, who without reasonable cause or excuse abandons it, whether permanently or not, in circumstances likely to cause it unnecessary suffering is guilty of an offence of cruelty. Equally, it is an offence to cause or procure such abandonment or, being the owner of the dog, to permit it.

Carriage of Dogs

A person who conveys a dog in such manner or position as to cause it any unnecessary suffering is guilty of an offence of cruelty. Likewise if he causes or procures such a conveying or, being the dog's owner, if he permits it.

Dogs as Draught Animals

A person who uses a dog to draw, or help to draw, any cart, carriage, truck or barrow on any highway is guilty of an offence. Likewise if he causes or procures such use or, being the dog's owner, if he permits it. For the meaning of "highway", see page 47.

Drugs and Poisons

If any person intentionally and without reasonable cause or excuse:

(a) administers any poisonous or injurious drug or substance to a dog; or

(b) causes or procures the administration of such drug or substance; or

(c) being the dog's owner, permits such administration; or

(d) causes any poisonous or injurious substance to be taken by a dog,

he is guilty of an offence of cruelty.

Experiments

The carrying out of an experiment on any living vertebrate animal which causes pain, suffering, distress or lasting harm is illegal unless the experiment is approved by licences issued by the Home Secretary. The licensing procedure, now operated under the Animals (Scientific Procedures) Act 1986, is stricter than that formerly operating under the repealed Cruelty to Animals Act 1876.

Dogs are not to be used for experiments unless supplied by an approved breeding establishment.

Experiments on animals forming part of exhibitions to the public or shown live on television for general reception are illegal. It is also an offence to advertise such experiments.

Fighting and Baiting

It is an offence of cruelty for any person:

(a) to cause, procure or assist at the fighting or baiting of a dog; or

(b) to keep, use, manage, or act or assist in the management of, any premises or place for the purpose, or partly for the purpose, of fighting or baiting a dog; or

65

(c) to permit any premises or place to be kept, managed or used for those purposes; or

(d) to receive, or cause or procure any person to receive, money for the admission of any person to such premises or place.

It is also an offence to keep or use, or act in the management of, any house, room, pit or other place for the purpose of fighting or baiting a dog. Persons attending dog fights without reasonable excuse, or advertising such fights, will commit offences and may be fined.

Operations and Anaesthetics

Any person who subjects a dog to an operation which is performed without due care and humanity is guilty of an offence of cruelty, as is anyone who causes or procures such an operation or, being the dog's owner, permits it.

With the exceptions mentioned below, all operations on dogs, with or without instruments, which involve interference with their sensitive tissues or bone structure, without the use of anaesthetics administered so as to prevent any pain during the operation are deemed to be operations performed without due care and humanity, and are consequently within the ambit of the last paragraph and are offences of cruelty. The exceptions are:

(a) the making of injections or extractions by means of a hollow needle;

(b) the rendering in emergency of first aid for the purpose of saving life or relieving pain;

(c) the docking of a dog's tail, or the amputation of its dew claws, before its eyes are open;

(d) any minor operation performed by a vet which by reason of its quickness or painlessness is customarily

66

performed without an anaesthetic, or any minor operation, whether performed by a vet or not, which is not customarily performed by a vet only; but castration is excluded from these operations.

The Government is empowered to make orders extending the classes of operations in which anaesthetics must be used.

Other Cases of Cruelty

An offence of cruelty is committed by a person if he cruelly:

(a) beats, kicks, ill-treats, tortures, infuriates or terrifies a dog; or

(b) causes or procures or, being the owner, permits a dog to be so used; or

(c) by wantonly or unreasonably doing or omitting to do any act, or causing or procuring the commission or omission of any act, causes any unnecessary suffering to a dog; or

(d) being the dog's owner, permits any unnecessary suffering to be caused as last described.

It will be seen that it is a necessary ingredient of these offences that the acts described be done cruelly. An act will be held to be done cruelly if pain or suffering is inflicted without good reason, and if the act is an unnecessary abuse of the dog. It will be immaterial that the accused had no intention to commit cruelty, except that, where the charge is one of causing or procuring, guilty knowledge must be shown.

Consequences of Conviction for Offences of Cruelty

In addition to fining and/or imprisoning offenders for offences of cruelty, the court has a number of other powers.

First, the court may, if satisfied that it would be cruel to keep the dog alive, direct that it be destroyed and assign it to any person for that purpose; but no such direction shall be given except upon the evidence of a registered vet unless the dog's owner assents. The court may order the owner to pay the reasonable expenses of destroying the dog. The court's direction is not appealable.

The court may also, in addition to any other punishment, deprive the offender of the ownership of the dog and may order its disposal, but only if it is shown by evidence as to a previous conviction or as to the character of the owner or otherwise that the dog, if left to him, is likely to be exposed to further cruelty. Furthermore, conviction for a cruelty offence enables the court to disqualify the offender for a stated period from having custody of a dog or of any other animal of a particular kind. Breach of a disqualification order is an offence which may lead to a fine and/or imprisonment.

Disqualification may be suspended by the court for so long as it thinks necessary for arrangements to be made for the alternative custody of the dog involved, or to allow an appeal to be made to the Crown Court. After 12 months from the date of disqualification the offender may apply to the court to remove it. If unsuccessful, he must wait at least 12 months before applying again, and so on for subsequent applications. Instead of refusing or granting the application, the court may vary the order to make it apply to a different kind of animal. When considering an application, the court will have regard to the applicant's character, his conduct since disqualification, the nature of the offence and any other circumstances of the case.

For any of the offences described, whether of cruelty or not, the court may order the offender to pay compensation of up to £2000 for any loss or damage resulting from that offence. This does not affect punishment for the offence but may affect damages awarded in civil proceedings.

A disqualification by the court from having the custody of a dog (or of other animals) has a further effect. A person so disqualified cannot obtain a licence to keep a pet shop, boarding kennels or dog breeding kennels (for which see Chapters 2 and 11) or riding stables. A person holding a licence for any of these establishments who is convicted of any offence under the Protection of Animals Act 1911 (or the corresponding Scottish Act) may have his licence cancelled by the court who may also disqualify him from keeping the kind of establishment to which his licence relates.

Chapter 14

Performing Dogs

The exhibition of performing animals at any entertainment to which the public is admitted, whether on payment or not, and the training of performing animals for such exhibitions, are controlled by the Performing Animals (Regulation) Act and the Performing Animals Rules, both of which originated in 1925. No definitions of "performing" or "performing animal" are attempted, but all animals are included except invertebrates.

The basis of this control is registration with the county or metropolitan district council backed up by powers to inspect the animals and the places where they are kept and sanctions by the court. (In London, registration is with the City Corporation or the borough council.) The person exhibiting or training animals should register with that one of these authorities within whose area he lives.

The training of animals for bona fide military, police, agricultural or sporting purposes, and the public exhibition of animals so trained, are exempted from registration. No definition of any of these terms in this context is available and, apart from gun dogs and sheep dogs, the scope of agricultural and sporting purposes seems to be limited.

Applications for registration must contain particulars of the animals and of the general nature of the performances for which they are to be exhibited or trained. A fee, as fixed by the registration authority, must accompany the application.

The authority appears to have no discretion to refuse registration provided the application is correctly made out and the fee paid, unless the applicant is disqualified from registration, for which see page 72. A certificate of registration is issued. It will contain the particulars on the application form, and they will also be entered on the authority's register, which is open to inspection. An applicant may later apply to have these particulars varied, when the authority will cancel the existing certificate and issue a new one without charging a further fee.

If a magistrates' court is satisfied on a complaint made by the police or an officer of the registering authority that the training or public exhibition of any performing animal has been accompanied by cruelty and should be prohibited or allowed only subject to conditions, the court may make an order accordingly. There is a right of appeal to the Crown Court. The order comes into force 7 days after it is made or, if an appeal is lodged within that time, when the appeal is determined but subject, of course, to the outcome of the appeal. Particulars of the order will be endorsed on the issued certificate and entered in the authority's register.

Police officers and authorised officers of the registering authority have power to enter premises, and to inspect them and performing animals there, but may not go on or behind the stage during a public performance.

Offences punishable by fine have been created if a person does any of the following things:

(a) exhibits or trains (in the terms described at the beginning of this Chapter) a performing animal without being registered unless he is exempted, or does so outside the terms of registration;

(b) fails to comply with an order of the magistrates' court;

(c) obstructs or deliberately delays an officer when exercising his powers of entry and inspection;

(d) conceals any animal to avoid its inspection;

(e) fails to produce his certificate to the court for endorsement;

(f) applies to be registered when disqualified by a court for registration.

When a person is convicted of any of these offences, or of offences against the Protection of Animals Act 1911 (for which, see Chapter 13), the convicting court may, as well as or instead of fining the offender:

(a) if he is registered under the Performing Animals (Regulation) Act 1925, order that his name be removed from the register; and

(b) order him to be disqualified from being registered, either permanently or for such time as the order may stipulate.

The same provisions about appeal, the effective date of the order and the recording of the order as apply to an order made after a complaint of cruelty (for which see page 71) will apply to the orders described above.

Films

The Cinematograph Films (Animals) Act of 1937 is concerned with the depiction of scenes involving cruelty to dogs and many other kinds of domestic and captive animals. Briefly, it is an offence, punishable with fine or imprisonment or both, to exhibit to the public any film if in connection with its production any scene represented in the film was organised or directed in such a way as to involve the cruel infliction of pain or terror on an animal or the cruel goading of an animal to fury.

Chapter 15

DOGS AND GAME

It is not perhaps widely known that the pursuit of game by a dog and associated activities are as much subject to the game laws as the shooting of game with guns. There are four branches of the game laws to be looked at: prohibited times for taking game, poaching, game licences and the protection of game from dogs. The statutes involved are principally the Game Act of 1831, the Game Licences Act of 1860 and the Ground Game Act of 1880.

The laws about deer are not considered here.

Prohibited Times for Taking Game

Certain game birds are protected by close seasons. These are as follows, all dates being inclusive:

Black game	11th December to 19th August, except in Somerset, Devon and that part of the New Forest which lies in Hampshire where it is 11th December to 31st August.
Bustard or wild turkey	2nd March to 31st August.
Grouse or red game	11th December to 11th August.
Partridge	2nd February to 31st August.
Pheasant	2nd February to 30th September.

It is an offence to kill or take these birds during the above times. This means that they must not be killed or captured by any means, and tame game and carcases of game are included.

The killing by a dog or the use of a dog for the purpose of killing or taking some kinds of game on a Sunday or on Christmas Day is also prohibited. The kinds concerned are hares, pheasants, partridges, grouse, heath or moor game, and black game. As well as an actual killing by a dog, the use of a dog to put up game, to retrieve it or to point at it is consequently an offence on those days.

Poaching

Nineteenth Century statutes have created several offences to deal with poaching, both by day and night. Each varies in some manner from the other. The birds and animals which are the subject of the offences collectively are: hares, pheasants, partridges, grouse, heath or moor game, black game, woodcock, snipe, rabbits and bustards.

These matters are mentioned here because dog owners may often not appreciate the wide scope of these laws. Basically, a poacher is a person pursuing game when he has no right to it, and that right can only be obtained through occupation or ownership of land or by a document granting the right. The nature of the land is immaterial, and a member of the public has no more right to game on, say, roadside verges than he has to it on "private land". A person may poach with a dog as much as with a gun or snare. And lastly, though some offences require the taking or killing of game, others are committed simply by being on land in search or pursuit of game.

Game Licences

The combined effect of the Acts of 1831 and 1860 is that, subject to the exceptions mentioned below, a game licence is required to use a dog for the purpose of searching for, killing or pursuing game, or to assist in any manner in the taking, killing or pursuing of game by the use of a dog. Game in this context is woodcock, snipe, rabbits, hares, pheasants, partridges, grouse, heath or moor game, and black game.

Additionally to this wide requirement for a licence, it has been held that to walk about unlicensed with a dog where there is game is evidence of the commission of an offence. And it is up to anyone caught with game in his possession to prove that he acquired it innocently, i.e., in circumstances in which a licence was not needed.

However, the exceptions to the requirement provide a number of useful instances in which a game licence is not needed, and those which are relevant to dogs are:

(a) Rabbits may be taken by the owner of the land on which they are (except, apparently, on open land such as heath and moorland), and by a tenant of any land either by himself or by someone acting with his direction or permission.

(b) Hares may be taken on "enclosed lands" (probably meaning fields enclosed by hedges, fences and the like) by the occupier, by the owner of those lands who has the right of taking hares there, and by a person who is authorised by the occupier or such an owner, but in no case at night (one hour after sunset to one hour before sunrise). The authorisation must be in writing, stating the name of the authorised person, giving a description of the lands in question, and must be signed by the person giving it and witnessed.

(c) Under a further and rather similar exception, hares

and rabbits may be taken by the occupier of any land. He may also authorise certain people to take those animals and, if properly authorised, they will not need a game licence. They are:

(i) any number of members of the occupier's household resident on the land in his occupation;

(ii) any number of people in the occupier's "ordinary service" on the land – this probably means regular service;

(iii) one other person *bona fide* employed by the occupier for reward in the taking of hares and rabbits.

The authorisation must be in writing. No special form is required but it is sensible to include the particulars quoted at (b) above. In the case of moorlands and unenclosed non-arable land, except detached portions of either which are less than 25 acres in extent and adjoin arable lands, the rights of the occupier and of any authorised person (which rights are given by the Ground Game Act 1880) are by that Act suspended from 1st April to 31st August inclusive; and consequently the exemption from the game licence requirement will not operate for that period.

(d) Any person pursuing and killing hares, whether by coursing (organised or not) with greyhounds or by hunting with beagles or other hounds.

A further exception is provided for persons assisting in the taking of game, but they are precluded from using their own dogs or from lending the use of them to someone else.

A game licence is obtainable from Post Offices transacting money order business. Its cost will vary from £2 to £6, being dependent upon the length of time and the period of the year for which it is granted.

Protection of Game from Dogs

Although under the criminal law the Criminal Damage Act 1971 allows, subject to reservations, a person to kill or injure a dog to protect his property, the definition of "property" in the Act excludes game in a wild state.

The Act has the effect of allowing such action against a dog only if the game has been tamed, or is ordinarily kept in captivity, or is otherwise in the possession of a person, e.g., hand-reared and penned game birds. Further, the person taking such action is only justified in doing so if he believed that the game was in immediate need of protection and that the action taken was reasonable in the circumstances.

Even if there is justification as described, there is apparently no protection from civil proceedings, and a protector of game could face a claim from the dog's owner.

There is some rather ancient legal authority (two cases concerned with dog spears!) for saying that an occupier of land may take steps to protect his game in his absence. In modern times an occupier may be expected to be more circumspect. Spring traps may not be used against dogs, and devices such as spring guns and man traps which may kill or cause grievous bodily harm to a human trespasser are forbidden; but electrified wires are not, provided no injury is caused.

Chapter 16

IMPORT AND EXPORT

Import

The principal legislation involved with the import of dogs is the Animal Health Act of 1981 and the Rabies (Importation of Dogs, Cats and other Mammals) Order which was made in 1974. As a general rule, no dog may be imported into Great Britain until an import licence has been granted on behalf of the Minister of Agriculture, Fisheries and Food (in Scotland, the Scottish Secretary of State). But in two cases no licence is needed, as follows:

(a) When the dog has been in quarantine for at least 6 months or more in Northern Ireland, the Republic of Ireland, the Channel Islands or the Isle of Man.

(b) When the dog is landed with the intention of re-exporting it within 48 hours from the same port or airport. But satisfactory arrangements for its re-export must be made previously; otherwise its landing without a licence will be regarded as illegal.

The licence will require your dog to be detained and isolated, usually for 6 months from landing, at quarantine premises approved by the Minister or Secretary of State; however, it may be released earlier for immediate export.

The dog must be vaccinated with anti-rabies vaccine by the Veterinary Superintendent of the quarantine premises within 48 hours of its arrival there.

Importers of dogs are advised by the Ministry of Agriculture to take three steps beforehand:

(1) Reserve accommodation at approved quarantine

78

premises well in advance. A minimum of 4-8 weeks is recommended, with a longer period at holiday times; but see also (3), below. A list of these premises is obtainable from the Ministry at their Rabies Branch, Hook Rise South, Surbiton, Surrey KT6 7NF.

(2) Reserve the services of an authorised carrying agent. He will meet the dog at disembarkation, clear it through Customs and be responsible for its transport to the quarantine premises. If granted, the import licence will be sent to him. No other person may take possession of the dog during these stages of transit. A list of carrying agents authorised by the Ministry is obtainable from them at the above address.

(3) When you have received confirmation of the reservation of accommodation and of the carrier's services (as above), apply for an import licence on Form 1D 1. The Ministry advise that this should be done some time in advance, as indicated at (1) above. The form is obtainable from, and when completed should be sent to, the Ministry at the above address. If the dog is to be quarantined in Scotland, the Scottish Office Agriculture and Fisheries Department is involved instead of the Ministry of Agriculture; the former's address is Pentland House, 47 Robb's Loan, Edinburgh EH14 1TW.

The next steps are:

(a) The Ministry will confirm your bookings with the quarantine premises and the carrying agent.

(b) The Ministry will issue the licence to the carrying agent.

(c) The Ministry will send a "boarding document" to you or, if you are returning to Great Britain ahead of your dog, to your named representative abroad. This will confirm the licence number and act as written evidence which the shipper or airline will need to see before allowing the dog to be embarked or emplaned abroad.

(d) If you are arranging transport by air, the Minister will also send with the boarding document a red label to be handed to the airline for them to affix it to the crate containing the dog before it can be accepted abroad on the plane.

All expenses in connection with the landing, transit, quarantine and vaccination of your dog, and any claims for its loss, death or sickness, are matters for settlement between you and the person concerned with the particular matter. The Ministry and the Scottish Office will not be involved.

Dogs may be landed in Great Britain only at the following places:

Ports: Dover Eastern Docks; Harwich, Parkeston Quay; Hull; Portsmouth; Southampton.

Airports: Birmingham; Edinburgh; Gatwick; Glasgow; Heathrow; Leeds; Manchester; Norwich; Prestwick.

It is an offence, for which you may be prosecuted, to try to land your dog elsewhere, except in an emergency situation when the prior permission of a Diseases of Animals Inspector is needed.

Landing a dog without a licence is a more serious offence; if that happens, the dog will be directed to quarantine, re-exported or destroyed (whichever the owner chooses), and the expenses of so doing charged to him. A fine of up to £2000 may be imposed, and, where an intent to smuggle is proved, the maximum fine is unlimited and a sentence of imprisonment can also be given.

Whilst the granting of a licence is always discretionary, refusal is only likely when there is evidence of a false declaration in the application for it, or when the arrangements for its accommodation and carriage have not been confirmed (see items (1), (2) and (a) above).

There are also certain Customs' requirements to be met when a dog is imported. Its owner must make a declaration about the period of ownership abroad, change of residence and the animal's value. VAT, currently at 17.5%, will be charged on this value. Customs will need to see the declaration before releasing the dog to the carrying agent. Full details can be obtained from Customs and Excise, King's Beam House, Mark Lane, London E.C.3.

Export

If you want to export a dog, you will have to meet the requirements of the importing country's regulations. Enquiries about these should be made to the Export Section of the Ministry of Agriculture at the address given on page 79.

Generally, a British export licence is also necessary. Enquiries can be made of the Department of Trade, Export Licensing Branch, Millbank Tower, Millbank, London SW1P 4QU (Telephone 071-211-3000).

81

Index

Other books from Shaw & Sons

The following books can be purchased direct from Shaw & Sons Limited, 21 Bourne Park, Bourne Road, Crayford, Kent DA1 4BZ by sending a remittance for the price quoted which includes postage and packing. Alternatively, copies may be ordered from your local bookshop.

THE DOG LAW HANDBOOK
Godfrey Sandys-Winsch, *BA, Solicitor*

The first Part of this new work comprises the updated text of *Your Dog and the Law* which is extensively cross-referenced to the other Parts so that the text of the legislation and further explanations can be found easily.

Part 2 includes the text of the relevant sections of all Acts of Parliament relating to dogs that are currently in force, from the Night Poaching Act 1828 to the Dangerous Dogs Act 1991. Part 3 similarly carries the text of Acts relating to animals generally and Part 4 incorporates the text of all relevant Statutory Instruments and Regulations. These three Parts are annotated with explanations of the text, definitions and further references. The final Part consists of the text of Government Department circulars issued in respect of the new dangerous dogs legislation.

The book is designed for ease of use and comprehension by those outside the legal profession and will be a standard reference work for dog wardens in particular. Its loose-leaf format will allow the issue of supplements to keep it fully up-to-date as further legislative changes are made.

A5 looseleaf   1993   ISBN 0 7219 1340 7   328 pages   £35.00

ANIMAL LAW
2nd Edition
Godfrey Sandys-Winsch, *BA, Solicitor*

This book presents in a compact and comprehensive form the many facets of the law which affect those who have any sort of dealings with animals, whether their own or other people's.

Its wide survey of animal law spans topics ranging from the keeping of wild animals to the preservation of rare creatures, from the training of performing animals to the keeping of coypus, from straying animals to guard dogs, from the export of horses to the import of hares. The subject matter is presented in a simple and straightforward manner which makes easy reading for the layman.

Paperback   1984   ISBN 0 7219 0801 2   294 pages   £10.25

A GUIDE TO ANGLING LAW
R. Millichamp, *FIFM*

A clear, comprehensive explanation of fishery law, presented in a format which makes it an ideal source of information to the layman. This book will help anglers, fishery managers, riparian owners and others to find their way quickly through the legislation affecting fisheries.

The book is divided into two sections: the first covers the law in England and Wales, and the second covers the law in Scotland. The following subject areas are included: Fisheries Administration; Trespass; Pollution; Water Act 1989; Predators; Permits; Licences; Water Bailiffs; Unclean and Immature Fish; Salmon and Trout.

Paperback   1990   ISBN 0 7219 1240 0   186 pages   £9.95

GUN LAW
5th Edition
Godfrey Sandys-Winsch, *BA, Solicitor*

This book is devoted exclusively to the law relating to the use of guns. In it the ordinary person who handles guns will find all the requirements of the law which he needs to know, and those who have to enforce the law will find it an invaluable aid to them in their work.

The fifth edition incorporates recent developments such as the Firearms (Amendment) Act 1988, which introduced tighter controls on potentially lethal weapons, and will be of considerable value to lawyers, firearms dealers, sportsmen, landowners and gamekeepers, as well as the police and courts.

Paperback   1990   ISBN 0 7219 0363 0   202 pages   £9.50

HORSE LAW
J. Mackenzie, *Barrister*

A concise guide to the law affecting the horse owner, *Horse Law* provides valuable information for all those concerned with horses – including horse owners and riding school establishment proprietors. The work will also give both solicitors and barristers a clear introduction to the law of horse ownership.

The following subjects are covered in a readable, accessible style: Ownership; Buying and Selling; Riding Establishments; Negligence; Import, Export and Movement of Horses; Protection from Cruelty; Rights of Way; Road Traffic Law; Keeping a Horse.

Paperback   1990   ISBN 0 7219 1130 7   127 pages   £9.95